INTRODUCING INVERTEBRATES

Written by Graham Meadows & Claire Vial

CONTENTS

Dominie Press, Inc.

THE INVERTEBRATES

Invertebrates are animals that have no backbone. More than nine out of ten living animals are invertebrates. They are found all over the world, in almost every type of **habitat.** They range in size from single-celled animals to giant squid that weigh more than two **tons**.

There are many different groups of invertebrates. This book looks at a few of these groups, which are shaded green in the chart below.

Some invertebrates, such as jellyfish and worms, have soft bodies. Others, such as crabs and snails, have soft bodies protected by a hard shell.

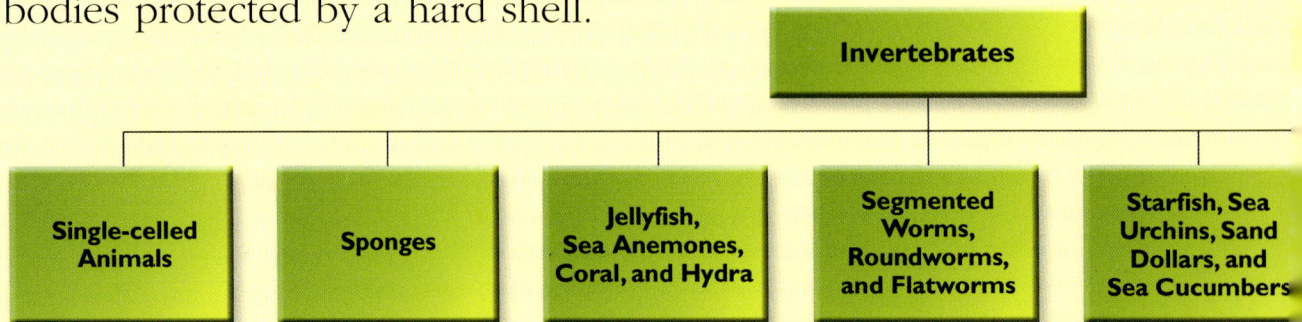

Invertebrates				
Single-celled Animals	Sponges	Jellyfish, Sea Anemones, Coral, and Hydra	Segmented Worms, Roundworms, and Flatworms	Starfish, Sea Urchins, Sand Dollars, and Sea Cucumbers

(Note: This chart does not show all the groups of invertebrates.)

◀ Warratah
Sea Anemone

▼ Leafveined
Slug

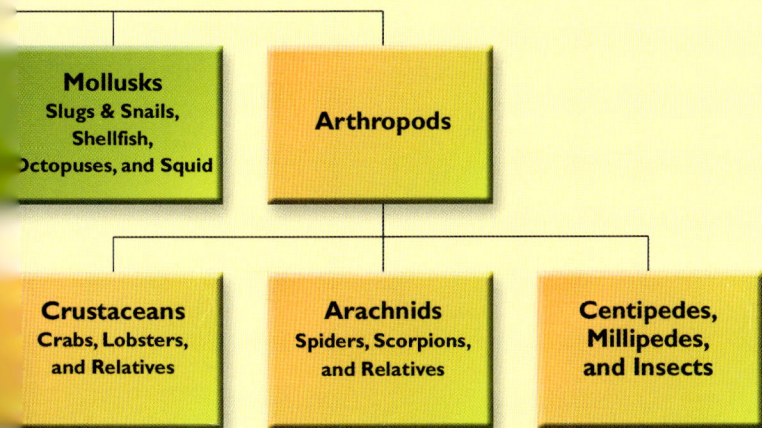

Mollusks	Arthropods
Slugs & Snails, Shellfish, Octopuses, and Squid	

Crustaceans	Arachnids	Centipedes,
Crabs, Lobsters, and Relatives	Spiders, Scorpions, and Relatives	Millipedes, and Insects

3

Amoeba ▶

Protozoan ▼

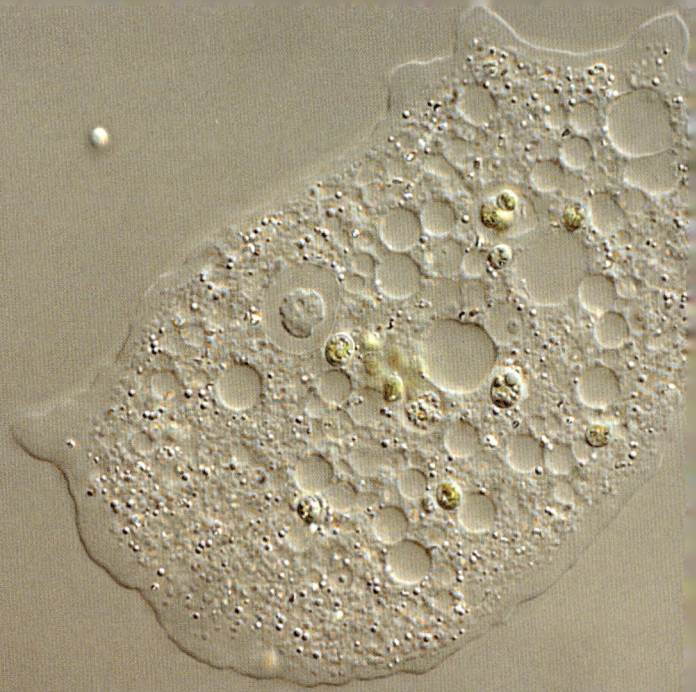

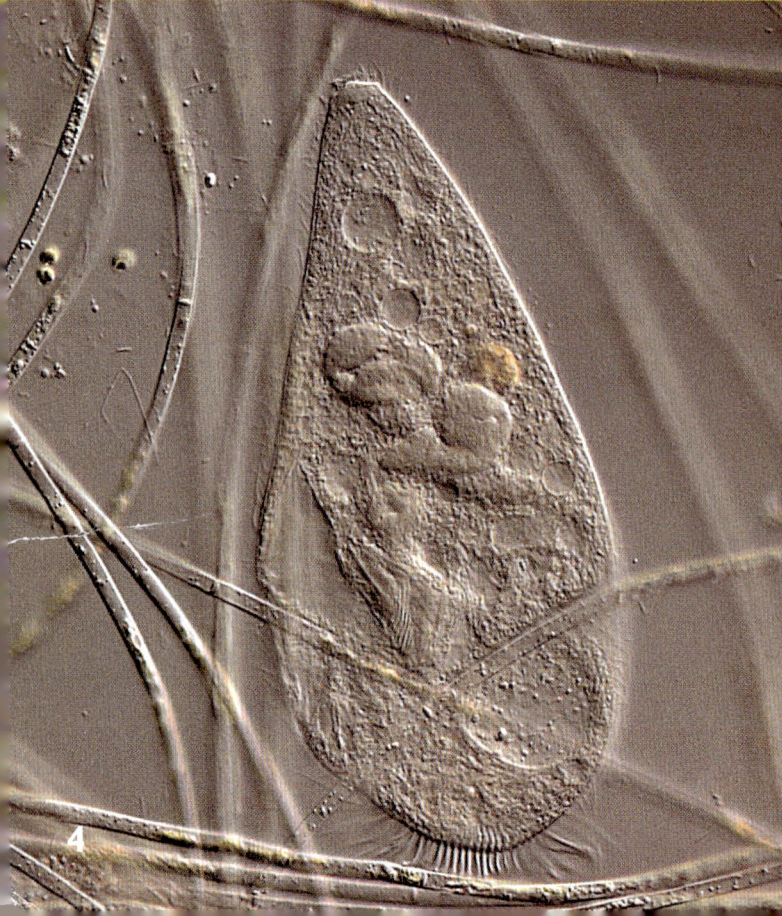

4

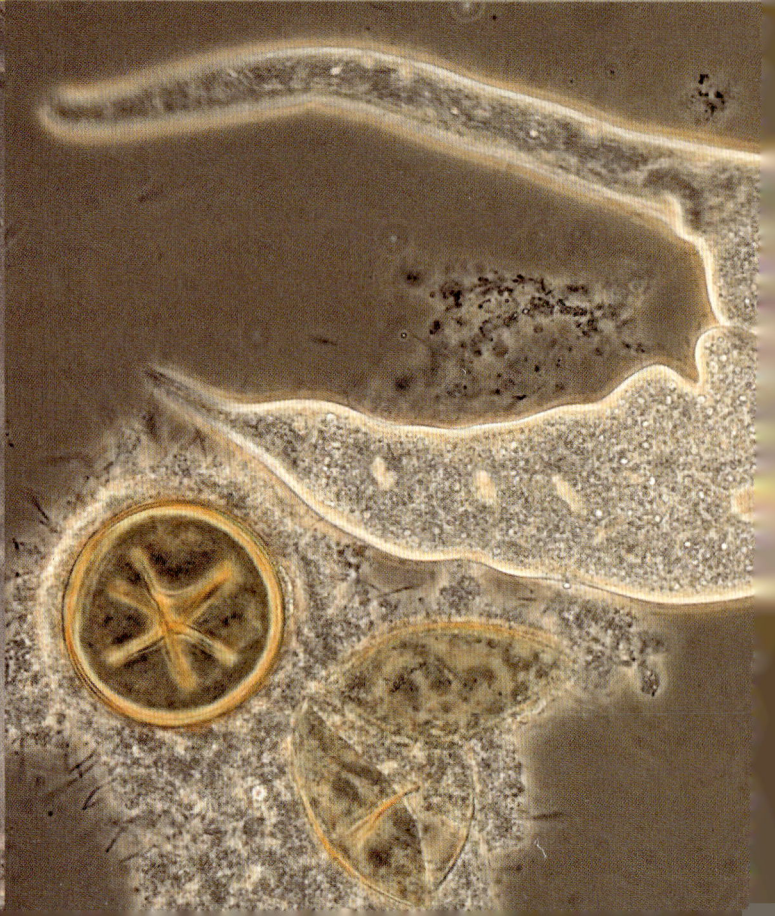

SINGLE-CELLED ANIMALS

Single-celled animals are called protozoa, which means "first animals." There are about 250,000 **species** of protozoa. Most are **microscopic**, which means they are too small to see with the human eye.

All single-celled animals need a moist **environment** to **survive**. They can be found in the sea, in freshwater habitats, and in moist soil. Some are **parasites** that live inside animals or plants. Some live in the freezing cold of the Arctic, and still others live in the waters of hot springs.

Some single-celled animals absorb food into their bodies. Some feed on plants. Others catch and eat other tiny animals, such as bacteria.

All single-celled animals can move. Some do this by changing shape; others swim.

◀ **Protozoan**

SPONGES

There are about 4,500 species of sponges, all of which are **aquatic**. Most types of sponges live in shallow sea-water, but some live as deep down as 2,700 feet. A few sponges live in freshwater habitats.

Some sponges live alone; others live in colonies. Most sponges stay in one place, but some creep slowly along. Sponges vary in shape, size, and color. Some are flat, some look like vases, and some have branches. Sponges range in size from a fraction of an inch to six feet high. They feed by sucking in water through holes in their sides and pushing it out through a hole at the top. They filter out tiny plants and animals.

◀ **Yellow Finger Sponge**

▲ **Flask Sponge**

Spotted Jellyfish ▶

Sunshine Coral ▶

JELLYFISH, CORALS, AND THEIR RELATIVES

All jellyfish, corals, and their relatives have arms, or tentacles, with special stinging cells. They are all **carnivores**. Some species live alone; others live in groups.

Jellyfish

Jellyfish are soft-bodied animals that float in water. Most live in the sea and have a body shaped like a bell or an umbrella. Around the edge of the body are long, often poisonous, tentacles.

Corals

Brain Coral ▲

Corals live in the sea. They have a special type of skeleton that contains calcium. There are two types of corals: stony coral, such as brain coral; and soft coral, such as sunshine coral.

Stony corals are the main type of coral that form **coral reefs**. Soft corals are more delicate and feathery in shape.

SEA ANEMONES

Sea anemones live in the sea. Most sea anemones have soft bodies and are shaped like a flower. They are usually attached to rocks, the sea floor, vegetation, or other animals.

▼ **Sea Anemone**

By-the-wind Sailor ▲

SEA FIRS AND HYDRAS

Most sea firs and hydras are **marine** animals, but some are found in fresh water. Some species attach themselves to rocks or vegetation. Others float in the water.

◀ **Sea Fir**

▲ Orange Marine Flatworm

◀ Tapeworm

WORMS

Worms are soft-bodied animals. There are many kinds of worms. Three of the best-known groups of worms are: flatworms, roundworms, and segmented worms.

Flatworms

This group includes flukes, tapeworms, and flatworms. Some are too small to be seen with the human eye.

Flukes and tapeworms are parasites. They live inside humans and animals. Some tapeworms can grow up to fifty feet in length.

Flatworms are not parasitic. They have a soft, flattened body covered with a special slime called mucus. They are found on land, in fresh water, and in salt water.

Flatworms ▶

Roundworms

Roundworms are shaped like a tube, and many are tapered at both ends. Many roundworms live in soil, fresh water, and the sea. Most are too small to be seen with the human eye.

Some roundworms are parasitic and live in humans, animals, or plants. Roundworms that live inside humans can grow to be eighteen inches long.

Segmented Worms

This group of worms includes earthworms, leeches, and many types of worms that live in the sea. Their bodies are made up of segments.

Segmented worms are found in the sea, in fresh water, and on land. They feed on plants and small animals.

▼ Red Worms

Roundworms ▼

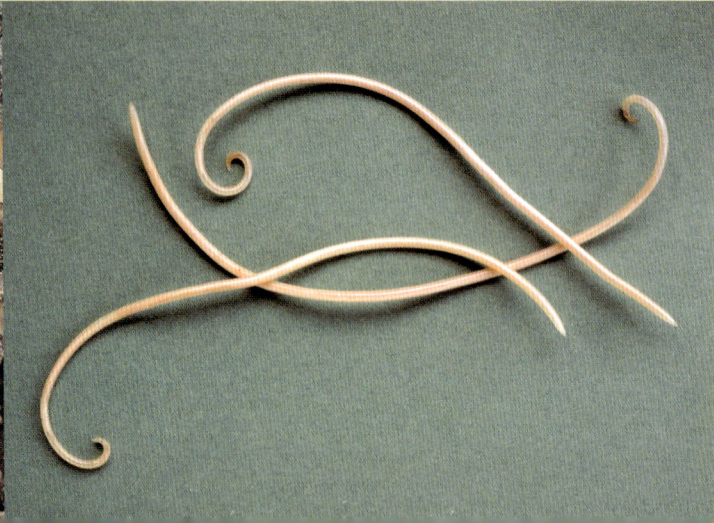

▲ **Christmas Tree Worms**

15

Sea Urchin ▲

STARFISH, SEA URCHINS, AND THEIR RELATIVES

All starfish, sea urchins, and their relatives are marine animals that live on the sea floor. Many species have bodies made up of five segments.

Starfish

Starfish, also called sea stars, have rough, hard skin. Most starfish have five arms, under which there are many tube feet. Starfish are carnivores. They feed on small animals, such as clams and oysters.

Sea Urchins

Sea urchins have a hard, round, outer shell. They have long, sharp spines for protection. In many species these spines contain poison. Between theses spines are tube feet.

Sea urchins are **omnivores**. Their **diet** includes plants and other animals.

Rose Starfish ▼

Starfish Arm ▲
with Tentacles

SAND DOLLARS

Sand dollars, also called sea biscuits, are flat and shaped like a disk. The disk is covered with very short spines. Between these spines are tube feet. Sand dollars are omnivores. They feed on plants and other animals found in sand or mud.

▲ Sand Dollar, or Sea Biscuit

SEA CUCUMBERS

Sea cucumbers have soft bodies that are shaped like a tube. They do not have a spine, but they do have tube feet. Sea cucumbers are omnivores. They have tentacles around their mouth. They use these tentacles to feed on plants and animals found in sand or mud. They also use their tentacles to catch small animals.

Tiger Tail Sea Cucumber ▲

▲ **Apple Sea Cucumber**

Apricot Sea Slug ▲

Garden Snail ▶

MOLLUSKS

Most mollusks have a hard external shell and a muscular foot. Most mollusk species live in the sea. Some live in fresh water, and others live on land.

Three well-known groups of mollusks are: slugs and snails, oysters and their relatives, and octopuses and their relatives.

Slugs and Snails

Some slugs and snails live in the sea, some live in fresh water, and others live on land. All slugs and snails have a muscular foot. Most have a visible shell. In some, such as the garden slug, the shell is very small and is hidden under the skin. Some slugs that live in the sea have no shell at all.

Giant Clam ▲

Oysters and Their Relatives

Oysters and their relatives include mussels, scallops, and clams. They have two shells, which are hinged together. They have a muscular foot. Some use their foot to creep along or to **burrow** into the sand.

Some scallops swim by opening and closing their shells. Clams, oysters, and mussels do not move around. They attach themselves to rocks. Most of them feed on small animals and plants in the water.

Octopuses and Their Relatives

Octopuses and their relatives include squid, cuttlefish, and nautiluses. They all have eight arms with suckers. Their suckers are used to catch animals. Most of them have a pair of large eyes.

▲ Octopus

◄ Cuttlefish

23

GLOSSARY

aquatic:	Living and growing in water
burrow:	To dig in the ground
carnivores:	Animals that eat other animals
coral reefs:	Natural underwater ridges made up of coral and minerals
diet:	The food that an animal or a person usually eats
environment:	Surroundings; the setting where animals or people live
habitat:	Areas where animals and plants live and grow
marine:	Relating to the sea
microscopic:	Very small; only visible through a microscope
omnivores:	Animals that eat both plants and other animals
parasites:	Animals that live on other animals and use them to survive
species:	Types of animals that have some physical characteristics in common
survive:	To stay alive and thrive
ton:	A measure of weight; one ton equals 2,000 pounds

INDEX